Th

The 1976 Lamont Poetry Selection
of The Academy of American Poets

The Academy of American Poets named its first
Lamont Poetry Selection in 1954. From 1954
through 1974 this distinguished award supported
the publication and distribution of twenty first
books of poetry. Since 1975 the Lamont Poetry
Selection has been given to an American poet
who has published one book in a standard edition,
insuring the publication of that poet's second
book of poems. Judges for 1976: Alan Dugan,
Michael S. Harper, Philip Levine.

Poems by Larry Levis

THE AFTERLIFE

Carnegie Mellon University Press
Pittsburgh 1998

Acknowledgements

I am grateful to the editors of the following magazines and anthologies in which these poems first appeared: *Choice:* The Morning After My Death; *Cincinnati Poetry Review:* In a Country; *Eureka Review:* The Invention of Maps; *Field:* A Poem of Horses, Linnets, Readings in French; *The Iowa Review:* The Map; *The New Yorker:* The Crimes of the Shade Trees, Inventing the Toucan; *The North American Review:* The Witness; *The Ohio Review:* Signs; *Open Places:* The Double, In Captivity, Rhododendrons; *Review La Booche:* Waking; *Three Rivers Poetry Journal:* Delwyn Creed; *Westigan Review:* Elegy.

"Inventing the Toucan" and "The Crime of the Shade Trees" © 1975 by The New Yorker Magazine, Inc. "Linnets" was published as a pamphlet, *The Rain's Witness*, by the Southwick Press in 1975. I am grateful to the National Endowment for the Arts for a Fellowship in 1973 which enabled me to complete many of the poems in this book.

Library of Congress Catalog Card Number 97-76758
ISBN 0-88748-279-1
Copyright © 1977 by Larry Levis
All rights reserved
Printed and bound in the United States of America

First Carnegie Mellon University Press Edition,
February 1998

The Afterlife was first published by The University of Iowa Press, Iowa City, in 1977.

The publisher would like to express his gratitude to
Barbara Cully, Philip Levine, Mary Flinn, and
Sheila Brady for their assistance in producing this volume.

Publication of this book is supported by gifts to the Classic Contemporaries Series from James W. Hall, Richard M. Cyert, and other anonymous benefactors.

Contents

For Marcia

I

Despues del amor, la tierra
Despues de la tierra, nadie.

Miguel Hernandez

Rhododendrons

WINTER has moved off
somewhere, writing its journals
in ice.

But I am still afraid to move,
afraid to speak,
as if I lived in a house
wallpapered with the cries of birds
I cannot identify.

Beneath the trees
a young couple sits talking
about the afterlife,
where no one, I think, is
whittling toys for the stillborn.
I laugh,

but I don't know.
Maybe the whole world is absent minded
or floating. Maybe the new lovers undress
without wondering how
the snow grows over the Andes,
or how a horse cannot remember those
frozen in the sleigh behind it,
but keeps running until the lines tangle,
while the dead sit coolly beneath their pet stars.

As I write this,
some blown rhododendrons are nodding
in the first breezes. I want

to resemble them, and remember nothing,
the way a photograph of an excavation
cannot remember the sun.

The wind rises or stops
and it means nothing.

I want to be circular;
a pond or a column of smoke
revolving, slowly, its ashes.

I want to turn back and go up
to myself at age 20,
and press five dollars into his hand
so he can sleep.
While he stands trembling on a street in Fresno,
suddenly one among many in the crowd
that strolls down Fulton Street,
among the stores that are closing,
and is never heard of again.

HE is swallowing beer
in the frozen vineyard
he uproots and burns —
clearing land for tract homes.

2. His Son
Eyes gleaming like something stolen,
he sneers at me and at the slick river
carrying shoe leather on its back.
On methedrine he doodles
halos, snakes, stars.

He dreams of making a coat,
of hunting alone above timberline
until he spits blood, and goes on
thanking no one, goes past
the ice inventing itself.

In the still air,
7,000 feet above the valley,
he brings down a wolf thin with disease,
loosens and counts the old teeth,
brushes snow from its eyes,
and talks softly. At home,
its silence enters him.
He skins it, slicing big loops
for the sleeves.
At night he buries the head

beyond the hen house,
and lets it dry. For days
he refuses to eat or speak.

Wearing wolf fur he waits to be fatherless.

3.
He waits for years while
his father spits and blinks into small fires.
And I lead these children in a flag salute
we finish in whispers.
I talk about nouns and verbs.

When Delwyn Creed married Sharon Bloodworth,
I was a child warming my hands
around the exhaust pipe of a Ford tractor—
and we drove the Koreans into the Arctic Sea,
and my brother snapped a rooster's neck
skillfully between his thumb and index finger
and turned and smiled slowly.

Elegy

AT the end
she laughed at get well cards,
at each of her dresses,
at her new shoes
filling with silence,
until there was nothing
to laugh at—and
the oak and the elm
filled with the night
a child might draw.

I stare past you at
the little white knobs
on a dresser which
will outlast us.
Like the knuckle
on the mammoth—
astonishing and
too stupid to live.

2.

You laugh at the thought
of God's hand so slick
by now and creased
with his failures: idiot,
clubfoot, doorstep,
pot on the stove boiling
over, your dead mother

you survive and bury.
'New Jersey,' her grave says,
and 'winter.'

You look in
the cup with lipstick stain.
You look and look.

The rain
and the still weeds
deeply rooted by now
tell you nothing.

   3.
A man in shirtsleeves
who pumps gas yawns
as we drive past
the black trunks of
almond trees.

Above Piedra
the river has thawed,
trout rise to lures,
the moon whitens.

   for R. P. C.

The Witness

IN the first freeze,
when the crystals of ice
begin singing,
the carp will not blink.

His gills open and close,
thoughtless.
He's an eye only,
a witness with a long stare,
a refusal.

And I have sat all night
in a hotel lobby
in Missouri
with still lips
slightly parted,
listening.

Is the snow
a birth?
How can a root
stand itself?
Or the born blind,
do they sing much?

*

I don't know.
Ask the heel
of your mother's shoe,
ask the rain
whose one syllable
becomes the voice

of your father
who stares up
from the couch.
Bend and kiss him.
Is his face
your own,
a shy paralysis
that attends birth?

The trees
he walked under
take him in,
he stops talking
to his father,
he stops talking.
The shadows
on the Sierras
go still,
the clouds
do not move.
He lies there.

Until he is blind
or childlike.

Or until it is 1943
and a woman watches
troops pass and smile
from a train. She turns
back to her stove,

to her stockings drying
on a radiator,
and forgets them,
dead in the long grasses.
    *
You sit in a chair
as the days pass.
The cliffs whole tribes
have abandoned
are yours. You think
the unborn grow
younger each second,
you crush a cigarette
under your heel
and walk out
as the unpicked fruit
darkens above you.

No one knows anything.

    2.
I woke and ate.
At the end
of the unfinished letter,
I stared at words
no one could have
fathered, until they
grew still and took on
the depth of woods,

the patience of ponds
blackening under
the flat shadows,
all the hearses
of shadows that ride
quietly as glass
placed over the eyelids
of the dead.

So I imagine
a delicate rain
is eating its way,
finally, into
every stranger I know.
And I walk out
into rain,
past the bars
filling with men,
past the palm reader's
and the thrift shop
where someone goes on
quietly polishing,
shining the shoes
of the dead
until they look
almost like new.

for Thomas McAfee

O U T here, I can say anything.
I can say, for example, that a girl
disappearing tonight
will sleep or stare out
fixedly as the train moves her
into its adulthood of dust
and sidings.
I remember watching wasps
on hot evenings
fly heavily over chandeliers
in hotel lobbies.
They've torn them down, too.
And the elderly drunks
who seemed not to mind anything,
who seemed to look for change
in their pockets, as they gazed
at the girl in the Pepsi ad,
and the girl who posed for the ad,
must all be dead now.

I can already tell that this
is no poem to show you,
this love poem. It's so
flat spoken and ignorable,
like the man chain smoking
who discovers he's
no longer waiting for anyone,
and goes to the movies

alone each Saturday, and grins,
and likes them.
This poem so like the hour
when the street lights turn
amber and blink, and the calm
professor burns another book,
and the divorcee waters her one
chronically dying plant.
This poem so like me
it could be my double.

I have stood for a long time
in its shadow, the way I stood
in the shadow of a dead roommate
I had to cut down from the ceiling
on Easter break, when
I was young.

That night I put my car
in neutral, and cut the engine
and lights to glide downhill
and hear the wind rush over
the dead metal.
I had to know what it felt
like, and under the moon,
gaining speed, I wanted to slip
out of my body and be
done with it.

A man can give up smoking
and the movies, and live for years
hearing the wind tick over roofs
but never looking up from
his one page, or the tiny
life he keeps carving over and
over upon it. And when everyone
around him dies, he can move
a grand piano into
his house, and sit down
alone, and finally play,
certain that no one will
overhear him, though he plays
as loud as he can,
so that when the dead come
and take his hands off the keys
they are invisible, the way air
and music are not.

Signs

ALL night I dreamed of my home,
of the roads that are so long
and straight they die in the middle—
among the spines of elderly weeds
on either side, among the dead cats,
the ants who are all eyes, the suitcase
thrown open, sprouting failures.

2.

And this evening in the garden
I find the winter
inside a snail shell, rigid and
cool, a little stubborn temple,
its one visitor gone.

3.

If there were messages or signs,
I might hear now a voice tell me
to walk forever, to ask
the mold for pardon, and one
by one I would hear out my sins,
hear they are not important—that I am
part of this rain
drumming its long fingers, and
of the roadside stone refusing
to blink, and of the coyote
nailed to the fence with its
long grin.

And when there are no messages
the dead lie still—
their hands crossed so strangely
like knives and forks after supper.

4.
I stay up late listening.
My feet tap the floor,
they begin a tiny dance
which will outlive me.
They turn away from this poem.
It is almost Spring.

II

YOU sail placidly down the Orinoco in a white dress.
You cross your legs and accept a drink from a stranger.
But then your mother and father, dragging the dead mule
Out of the shade, begin waving and calling.

You swim over and kneel beside the animal.
Speaking softly, you do not disturb the toucan,
Who dreams, on the branch just above you,
That his stripes have grown younger.

Your mother and father kneel behind you
And flutter their hands weakly as if in prayer, until
It seems you too are clutching a limb with huge claws,
As the skin over each knuckle hardens.

You grip deeply, until there is no future but this.
You think of your rented house trailer,
Of the smoke that is rising bashfully
Out of all the chimneys at once in Boise, Idaho.

But you suspect something.
The jungle is too green.
The mule's lips are becoming a little too intimate.
And these two aren't your real parents.

for M.

MY love and I are inventing a country, which we
can already see taking shape, as if wheels were
passing through yellow mud. But there is a prob-
lem: if we put a river in the country, it will thaw
and begin flooding. If we put the river on the bor-
der, there will be trouble. If we forget about the
river, there will be no way out. There is already a
sky over that country, waiting for clouds or smoke.
Birds have flown into it, too. Each evening more
trees fill with their eyes, and what they see we can
never erase.

One day it was snowing heavily, and again we were
lying in bed, watching our country: we could
make out the wide river for the first time, blue and
moving. We seemed to be getting closer; we saw
our wheel tracks leading into it and curving out
of sight behind us. It looked like the land we had
left, some smoke in the distance, but I wasn't sure.
There were birds calling. The creaking of our
wheels. And as we entered that country, it felt as if
someone was touching our bare shoulders, lightly,
for the last time.

APPLYING to Heavy Equipment School
I marched farther into the Great Plains
And refused to come out.
I threw up a few scaffolds of disinterest.
Around me in the fields, the hogs grunted
And lay on their sides.

You came with a little water and went away.
The glass is still on the table,
And the paper,
And the burned scaffolds.

   *

You were bent over the sink, washing your stockings.
I came up behind you like the night sky behind the town.
You stood frowning at your knuckles
And did not speak.

   *

At night I lie still, like Bolivia.
My furnaces turn blue.
My forests go dark.
You are a low range of hills, a Paraguay.
Now the clouds cover us both.
It is raining and the movie houses are open.

Waking

YOU could hear someone arguing
About money, a man and his wife.
You could hear them closing the little jails

No one would enter or sweep.
The inmates were thinking of water.
They would sleep standing up,

If they had to. All that summer,
Outside, you could hear
The freight cars move slowly.

When they passed, you would listen
To anything: to the counsel
Of a moth dying on the sill,

To the wind that had nothing
To say, that went on.
You loved the wind,

You loved the blackboards,
Where the equations died of perfection,
And the parables were burned herons,

Extinct. Each night you could feel
The migrations of shadows.
And you knew you had killed

No one: not your father or mother
Who sat watching TV; not your wife
Who wept and would not eat;

Not your brother who kept smiling.
You were their stranger.
You were the widow of sleep.

2.
You were a kite of ashes falling
And spreading in air.
There was no one below you.

And the Pyramids would not awaken.
The lost tribes would starve
And the jungle would be greener

Without them. The extinct
Froze into maps of ice.
You loved falling;

You loved the braille
Of starfish and the snows,
High and fatherless.

You loved fire,
And the hail that had no memory.
You loved to forget.

3.
You wake in a hotel,
In the custody of rats' eyes
Where the small wheels of clocks

Move intricately as ice or the prayers
You will not say. You knew
You would leave.

It would rain
And you would lie
In bed all day wondering

Who fathered the air.
You would listen to your own breath
And think it was no one's.

4.
You think of snow,
The blank page that forgets us,
The strangers we grow into.

Sometimes we burn so cleanly
There is nothing left.
There is the hotel in the rain,

The man and his wife arguing,
The mastodon's stillness,
The migrations of birds.

5.
The starfish is dreaming of snow.
Your father and mother sleep
And the trees inhale the light.

L O O K I N G into the eyes of Gerard de Nerval
You notice the giant sea crabs rising.
Which is what happens
When you look into the eyes of Gerard de Nerval,
Always the same thing: the giant sea crabs,
The claws in their vague red holsters
Moving around, a little doubtfully.

2.
But looking into the eyes of Pierre Reverdy
Is like throwing the editorial page
Out into the rain
And then riding alone on the subway.

Also, it is like avoiding your father.
You are hiding and he looks for you
Under each vine; he is coming nearer
And nearer. What can you do
But ignore him?

3.
In either case, soon you are riding alone on a subway.
Which is not important.
What is important is to avoid
Looking too closely into the eyes of your father,
That formal eclipse.

IS it raining on a lame mare
About to be shot?

The horse goes down quickly,
Its legs twitching.
Later they will stiffen.

After the rain stops
The gnats go in and out of its ears,
Which are cool, two dreamer's gloves,
When I touch them.

   2.
They were going to skin it, as usual.
Hoisting it up full length
Behind a truck
And stripping it with knives
Until the white skin
Showed plainly as a map spread
In a general's tent—
His index finger naming the little towns
To be taken before dawn.

YOUR friends nod. Their glances are like huts
In which tools have been abandoned.
Maybe you have already begun dying.
Someone bumps into you and it takes root,
A low shrub, disinterested.

So you work late in an office building
While a man vacuums the floors.

You go further into the blank paper.
You go past the white smirk of the benign.
You find the dark trousers of your father,
The hairpins of your mother.
You hold them in your hands,

While the jails are closing in Santiago
And the sores on the gelding's withers
Are ordinary. They glisten in the rain
Outside the jail, and say nothing.

                *

It was 1946 and the war was over.
Your father hung his trousers on the bed.
Your mother undressed and shook out her hair.
They moved closer. As you began,
They blindfolded the horse and led him further
Up the cliff while the shadows
Pulled on their gloves one by one and went out,
And left them alone.

The Crimes of the Shade Trees

TODAY everyone forgave me.
No one mentioned the felony
Of my back against the oak,
Or the air I was breathing, earlier.
So it is possible I am not Levis.

I smoke and think possibly
I am the smoke—
Drifting through Omaha as smoke does,
Past the new sofas on sale.
Past the south view of the slaughterhouse,
And the shade trees flushing with light.

And it doesn't matter.
For example, if I am really
Something ordinary, a doorstep,
Or the gleaming of frost on someone's lawn
As he shaves, that would be all right.

I only mention this
To the caretaker of my absence,
Who dozes on a beige sofa.

While she knits us a bible
In which the blind remain blind,
Like shade trees. Filling with light,

Each leaf feels its way out,
Each a mad bible of patience.

MY body is a white thing in the sun, now.
It is not ashamed of itself,
Not anymore. Because today is
The morning after my death.
How little I have to say;
How little desire I have
To say it.

And these flies sleeping on doorsills
And hugging screens; and the child
Who has just run out of the house
After touching my body, who knows,
Suddenly, how heavy a dead man is . . .

What can the sun do but keep shining?
Even though I don't especially need it
Anymore, it shines on the palm fronds
And makes them look older,
The way someone who writes a letter,
And then tears it up, looks suddenly older.

2.
Far off, a band is playing Souza marches.
And as the conductor, in his sun stained
Uniform, taps his baton for silence, and all
Around him the foliage is getting greener,
Greener, like the end of things,
One of the musicians, resting

His trumpet on his knee, looks around
A moment, before he spits and puts the horn
Into his mouth, counting slowly.

And so I think of the darkness inside the horn,
How no one's breath has been able
To push it out yet, into the air,
How when the concert ends it will still
Be there, like a note so high no one
Can play it, or like the dried blood inside
A dead woman's throat, when the mourners
Listen, and there is nothing left but these flies,
Polished and swarming frankly in the sun.

OVER the picnics
The dwarf star is eating the sun.
Each day it feasts on more light.
We were getting used to blank mirrors,
And snapshots of former aunts
Fossilizing in our hands.
But there's no closet like the night,

That urgent fur, and the stars
Afflicting themselves on the sky
As if at a nowhere wedding. Whenever
The lovers undress, they are
The white of calendars without days,
The white of trout multiplying,
And blank dice, thrown once,

And then never again.
The bottle thinks of the note inside it
As bacteria, an irritant,
And it desires emptiness; it would
Be filled with air, with sleep.
I am the ashes of somebody else.
I hiss and conspire,

But nothing ends.
We'll go on, as always, harvesting walnuts
On our hands and knees,
And die voicelessly
As a sedan full of cigar smoke

Sinking under a bridge.
We'll turn slowly, flowers

In the mouths of drowned cattle.
In a dawn of burned fields,
The sun disappoints you,
And the blight you begin to remember
Is me.
Like an Alp overlooking a corpse,
I explain nothing:

The conductor leans
Out of his train; he watches
The water snakes gliding
Over the pond;
The moth sleeps on your coat
As you walk through the turnstile
And disappear.

Remember the spider drowsing
Under its clouds?
By now the dead flies surround her.
Her web is finished.
So think of silk.
Think of a long rain
You glanced at, once, through a window,

And turned back, opening this book,
This smoldering closet, in a house
Where you only came to play,

And where no one was ever at home.
But now, face down on the table,
There are dark cards,
And the place is on fire.

III

The Rain's Witness

ONE morning with a 12 gauge my brother shot
what he said was a linnet. He did this at close range
where it sang on a flowering almond branch. Any-
one could have done the same and shrugged it off,
but my brother joked about it for days, describing
how nothing remained of it, how he watched for
feathers and counted only two gold ones which he
slipped behind his ear. He grew uneasy and care-
less; nothing remained. He wore loud ties and two
tone shoes. He sold shoes, he sold soap. Nothing
remained. He drove on the roads with a little hole
in the air behind him.

BUT in the high court of linnets he does not get
off so easily. He is judged and sentenced to pull me
on a rough cart through town. He is further pun-
ished since each feather of the dead bird falls around
me, not him, and each falls as a separate linnet, and
each feather lost from one of these becomes a lin-
net. While he is condemned to feel nothing ever
settle on his shoulders, which are hunched over and
still, linnets gather around me. In their singing,
they cleanse my ears of all language but that of
linnets. My gaze takes on the terrible gaze of song
birds. And I find that I too am condemned, and
must stitch together, out of glue, loose feathers,
droppings, weeds and garbage I find along the
street, the original linnet, or, if I fail, be condemned
to be pulled in a cart by my brother forever. We
are tired of each other, tired of being brothers like
this. The backside of his head, close cropped, is what
I notice when I look up from work. To fashion
the eyes, the gaze, the tongue and trance of a linnet
is impossible. The eyelids are impossibly delicate
and thin. I am dragged through the striped zoo of
the town. One day I throw down the first stillborn
linnet, then another, then more. Then one of them
begins singing.

AS my brother walks through an intersection the noise from hundreds of thin wings, linnet wings, becomes his silence. He shouts in his loud clothes all day. God grows balder.

4.

WHALES dry up on beaches by themselves.
The large bones in their heads, their silence,
is a way of turning inward.

Elephants die in exile.
Their tusks begin curling, begin growing
into their skulls.

My father once stopped a stray dog
with a 12 gauge, a blast in the spine.
But you see them on the roads, trotting through rain.

Cattle are slaughtered routinely.
But pigs are intelligent and vicious to the end.
Their squeals burn circles.

Mice are running over the freezing snow.
Wolverines will destroy kitchens for pleasure.
Wolverines are so terrible you must give in.

The waist of a weasel is also lovely. It slips away.

The skies under the turtle's shell are birdless.

        *

These shadows become carp rising slowly. The black
trees are green again. The creeks are full
and the wooden bridge trembles.

The suicides slip beneath you, shining.
You think if you watched them long enough
you would become fluent in their ten foreign tongues

of light and drummed fingers and inbreedings.

SNAKES swallow birds, mice, anything warm.
Beaten to death with a length of pipe,
a snake will move for hours afterward, digesting.

In fact their death takes too long.
In their stillness it may be they outlast death.
They are like stones the moment after

a wind passes over.
The tough skin around a snake's eyes
is ignorant and eternal.

They are made into belts and wallets.
Their delicate meat can be eaten.
But you can't be sure.

In the morning another snake lies curled
on the branch just over your head.

*

Under the saint's heel in the painting,
a gopher snake sleeps.
The saint's eyes are syphilitic with vision.

He looks the Lord in the face.
He is like the bridge the laborers shrug at
as they wade across the water at night.

When LaBonna Stivers brought a 4 foot bullsnake
to High Mass, she stroked its lifted throat;
she smiled: 'Snakes don't have no minds.'

YOU can't be sure. Your whole family
may be wiped out by cholera. As the plums
blossom, you may hang yourself.

Or you may love a woman whose low laugh
makes her belly shake softly.
She wants you to stay, and you should have.

   *

Or like your brother, you may go
into the almond orchard to kill
whatever moves. You may want to go

against the little psalms and clear gazings
of birds, against yourself, a 12 gauge
crooked negligently over your shoulder.

You're tired of summer.
You want to stop all the singing.
And everything is singing.

At close range you blow a linnet
into nothing at all, into the silence
of stumps, where everyone sits and whittles.

   *

Your brother grows into a stranger.
He walks into town in the rain.
Two gold feathers behind his ear.

He is too indifferent to wave.
He buys all the rain ahead of him,
and sells all the silence behind him.

I THOUGHT when finished
it would break into flight, its beak
a Chinese trumpet over the deepest lakes.
But with each feather it grows colder to the touch.
I attach the wings which wait for the glacier
to slide under them. The viewpoint of ice
is birdless. I close my eyes,
I give up.

    *

I meet my brother in Los Angeles.
I offer him rain
but he clears his throat.
He offers me
the freeway and the sullen huts;
the ring fingers stiffening;
the bitten words.

There are no birds he remembers.
He does not remember owning a gun.
He remembers nothing of the past.

He is whistling 'Kansas City'
on Hollywood Boulevard, a bird
with half its skull eaten away
in the shoebox tucked under his arm.

    *

When the matinee ends, the lights come on
and we blink slowly

and walk out. It is the hour
when the bald usher
falls in love.

*

When we are the night and the rain,
the leper on his crutch will spit once,
and go on singing.

YOUR family stands over your bed
like Auks of estrangement.
You ask them to look you in the eye,
in the flaming aviary.
But they float over in dirigibles:

in one of them
a girl is undressing; in another
you are waking your father.

Your wife lies hurt on the roadside
and you must find her.
You drive slowly, looking.

They lift higher and higher
over the snow on the Great Plains.
Goodbye, tender blimps.

AT the end of winter
the hogs are eating abandoned cars.
We must choose between Jesus and seconal
as we walk under the big, casual spiders whitening
in ice, in tree tops. These great elms rooted in hell
hum so calmly.

My brother marching through Prussia
wears a chrome tie and sings.
Girls smoothing their dresses
become mothers. Trees grow more deeply
into the still farms.

The war ends.
A widow cradles her husband's
acetylene torch,
the flame turns blue,
a sparrow flies out of the bare elm
and it begins again.

I'm no one's father.
I whittle a linnet out of wood until
the bus goes completely dark around me.
The farms in their white patients' smocks join hands.
Only the blind can smell water,
the streams moving a little,
freezing and thawing.

     *

In Illinois one bridge is made entirely
of dead linnets. When the river sings under them,
their ruffled feathers turn large and black.

IT'S March; the arthritic horses
stand in the same place
all day.
A piebald mare flicks her ears back.

Ants have already taken over
the eyes of the house finch
on the sill.

So you think someone
is coming,
someone already passing the burned mill,
someone with news of a city
built on snow.

But over the bare table
in the morning
a glass of water goes blind
from staring upward.

For you
it's not so easy.
You begin the long witnessing:
Table. Glass of water. Lone crow
circling.

You witness the rain for weeks
and there are only the two of you.
You divide yourself in two and witness yourself,
and it makes no difference.

*

You think of God dying of anthrax
in a little shed, of a matinee
in which three people sit
with their hands folded and a fourth
coughs. You come down the mountain.

UNTIL one day in a diner in Oakland
you begin dying.
It is peace time.
You have no brother.
You never had a brother.
In the matinees no one sat next to you.
This brother for whom
you have been repairing linnets all your life,
unthankful stuffed little corpses,
hoping they'd perch behind glass in museums
that have been leveled, this brother
who slept under the fig tree
turning its dark glove inside out at noon, is no one;
the strong back you rode while
the quail sang perfect triangles, was no one's.
Your shy father extinct in a single footprint,
your mother a stone growing a cuticle.
It is being suggested that you were never born, that
it never happened in linnet feathers
clinging to the storm fence along the freeway;
in the Sierra Nevadas,
in the long azure of your wife's glance,
in the roads and the standing water,
in the trembling of a spider web gone suddenly still,
it never happened.

THIS is a good page.
It is blank,
and getting blanker.
My mother and father
are falling asleep over it.
My brother is finishing a cigarette;
he looks at the blank moon.
My sisters walk gravely in circles.
My wife sees through it, through blankness.
My friends stop laughing, they listen
to the wind in a room in Fresno, to the wind
of this page, which is theirs,
which is blank.

They are all tired of reading,
they want to go home,
they won't be waving goodbye.

When they are gone,
the page will be crumpled,
thrown into the street.
Around it, sparrows will be feeding
on bits of garbage.
The linnet will be singing.
A man will awaken on his deathbed,
not yet cured.

I will not have written these words,
I will be that silence slipping around the bend
in the river, where it curves out of sight among weeds,
the silence in which a car backfires and drives away,
and the father of that silence.

Carnegie Mellon
Classic Contemporaries

Peter Balakian
Sad Days of Light

Marvin Bell
The Escape into You
Stars Which See, Stars Which Do Not See

Kelly Cherry
Lovers and Agnostics

Andrei Codrescu
License to Carry a Gun

Deborah Digges
Vesper Sparrows

Stephen Dobyns
Black Dog, Red Dog

Rita Dove
Museum
The Yellow House on the Corner

Stephen Dunn
Full of Lust and Good Usage
Not Dancing

Cornelius Eady
Victims of the Latest Dance Craze

Maria Flook
Reckless Wedding

Charles Fort
The Town Clock Burning

Tess Gallagher
Instructions to the Double

Brendan Galvin
Early Returns

Amy Gerstler
Bitter Angel

Edward Hirsch
For the Sleepwalkers

Colette Inez
The Woman Who Loved Worms

Denis Johnson
The Incognito Lounge

X. J. Kennedy
Nude Descending a Staircase

Greg Kuzma
Good News

Larry Levis
The Dollmaker's Ghost
The Afterlife

Thomas Lux
Sunday
Half Promised Land

Jack Matthews
An Almanac for Twilight

David Mura
After We Lost Our Way

Carol Muske
Skylight

Gregory Orr
Burning the Empty Nests

Dave Smith
The Fisherman's Whore

Elizabeth Spires
Swan's Island

Maura Stanton
Snow on Snow
Cries of Swimmers

Gerald Stern
Lucky Life
Two Long Poems

James Tate
Absences
The Oblivion Ha-Ha

Jean Valentine
Pilgrims

Ellen Bryant Voigt
The Forces of Plenty

James Welch
Riding the Earthboy 40

Evan Zimroth
Giselle Considers Her Future